INTRODUCTION
TO STATISTICAL IDEAS

for Social Scientsts

G. KALTON

CHAPMAN & HALL LTD
11 New Fetter Lane London EC4

First Published 1966
Reprinted 1969
Reprinted 1973
ⓒ*1966 by Graham Kalton*
Varityped by Josée Utteridge
Vari-typing Services
Printed in Great Britain by
Whitstable Litho, Straker Brothers Ltd
SBN 412 08460 0

Distributed in the U.S.A.
by Barnes & Noble, Inc.

PREFACE

In this monograph I have attempted to write a broad review of
statistics, with a strong emphasis on ideas rather than techniques.
Most statistics textbooks for non-statisticians give detailed des-
criptions of calculation procedures with the result that the ideas
tend to be submerged by the wealth of computational instruction.
I feel that the most important part of statistics for the social scien-
tist to learn is the statistical way of thought, and I have therefore
tried to highlight ideas by largely ignoring the problems of computation. In any event, I think that the alternative approach of providing a few standard techniques is of strictly limited value, because
the real world rarely matches the textbook simplicity; the narrow
view of the subject resulting from such slight knowledge, without
a real understanding of the principles, is likely to lead to misapplication of the techniques.

I have kept the monograph brief because I think a short treat-
ise has much to offer; in particular many social scientists requir-
ing an introduction to statistics are unlikely to have the time to
work through a full-length textbook, but they should be able to
read this short account. Its brevity does mean, however, that it
may be too concise for the totally uninitiated who also find the
mathematical style of argument difficult. (While I have kept the
level of mathematics down to a minimum, the style is mathematical
with symbols replaced by words.) For such readers, I hope the
monograph will serve a useful purpose if used in conjunction with
a textbook or course of lectures. For those with greater familiarity
with mathematical thinking, I hope this account will be able to
stand on its own as an introduction to statistics. I also hope that
it will act as a useful refresher for those who have learned elementary statistics at some time. For all classes of reader, I hope

Preface

that it will widen their understanding of the subject.

Finally, I would like to thank the Research Committee of the National Foundation for Educational Research who provided me with the initial stimulus to write this monograph. Also, I would like to express my thanks to the many people, particularly colleagues and students at the London School of Economics and Political Science, who have read the drafts and given helpful criticisms ; in this connection, I should like to make special mention of my colleague, Mr. R.W. Lewis. I should also like to thank the secretaries of the Statistics Department who cheerfully performed the task of typing the drafts.

G.K.

London School of Economics
August 1965

CONTENTS

Preface   *Page* iii

1. Introduction   1

2. Summary Statistics   5

   (a) Attributes   5

   (b) Variables   6

3. Sampling Errors   15

4. Testing Relationships   26

   (a) Significance Test for the Difference between   27
   Two Means

   (b) Testing for Association between Attributes   34

   (c) Testing for Association between Variables   38

   (d) Testing for Association between an Attribute   45
   and a Variable

5. Concluding Remarks   52

   Bibliography   54

   Index   57

1. INTRODUCTION

In the social sciences much of the research undertaken involves, at some stage, the collection of statistical information. For example, economists collect data on the proportion of a family's income that is spent on housing, sociologists on the housing conditions of immigrants, social psychologists on the attitudes of nurses towards their patients, and educational psychologists on the effectiveness of a teaching machine in teaching algebra to school children. To carry out such research projects, a knowledge of statistics is required.

The field of statistics covers the general design of the research project, and especially the method of selecting the individuals to be studied — the sample, together with the methods of analysing the information collected, and the presentation of the numerical results. The intention of this monograph is to present only the basic *ideas* underlying a variety of statistical methods used in analysing and presenting results ; the reader must refer elsewhere for a discussion of sample designs.* The discussion is kept at a non-mathematical level and, in addition, the calculations are kept artificially simple to avoid the necessity for discussing computational techniques ; from the books listed in the bibliography the interested reader can learn more about the methods and detailed calculations. In order to attain this simplicity, all the numerical data employed are hypothetical.

Many research projects are designed to test hypotheses. For example, we may want to test whether one teaching method produces different results from another ; because of the nature of statistical tests we start out with the hypothesis that there is no

---

* For sample survey designs see Stuart [20], Moser [16] and Kish [12] ; for experimental designs see Cox [4] and Cochran and Cox [3].

difference, and design an experiment to test this hypothesis. In
the simplest type of design we might take two groups of students,
subject one group to the first teaching method and the other group
to the second; the procedure would then be to test all the students
and record their scores. Comparison of the scores obtained by the
two groups would be the method of testing the hypothesis: here,
we are investigating whether there is a relationship between the
teaching methods and scores obtained on the test. In general,
testing a hypothesis is the same as testing the existence of a
relationship.

Some research projects, however, are not designed to test
hypotheses but only to estimate the characteristics of the group
under study; they aim at describing these characteristics and are
seldom concerned with relationships (though they may describe
a relationship rather than test its existence). For example, we
may conduct a survey to estimate the proportion of the population
in Greater London living in overcrowded conditions.

This leads to the frequently-drawn distinction between 'analytic' and 'descriptive' surveys. Since most surveys have both
analytic and descriptive components, the distinction is somewhat
blurred, but nevertheless it is of great importance for two main
reasons. First, analytic and descriptive surveys demand very
different types of sample design. Secondly, it proves useful in
distinguishing two types of statistical analysis: tests of significance are used for the analytic aspects of a survey while confidence intervals are used for the descriptive aspects.

No matter what type of survey is involved, however, the first
problem in statistical analysis is to find the most suitable method
of summarizing the information collected so as to bring out the
essence of the findings. Here it is useful to distinguish between
two types of statistical data — *attributes* and *variables* — since they
involve different summary measures. An attribute is a qualitative
non-numerical description; for example, a person may be male or
female; single, married, widowed or divorced; may live in a house,
live in a flat, or in a student hostel. A variable, on the other

hand, is a quantitative measurement to which a numerical value is assigned; for example, a person's age, height, or income. Variables can be reduced to attributes: a student's examination score may be simplified to pass or fail, a man's height to short (under 5' 6" say), medium (5' 6" but under 6' 3"), or tall (6' 3" or over). This reduction generally throws away information — it is no longer possible to tell whether a man is 5' 0" or 5' 5", he is just short — and must therefore be used with caution. Strictly speaking, the height example fits an intermediate category between attributes and variables which can be called 'ordered' attributes, for the heights go from small through medium to tall; the Registrar-General's Social Class grouping is also ordered, from Social Class I to Social Class V. On the other hand, attributes such as marital status, colour of hair, or the degree subjects taken by university students, do not fall in a special order, and can therefore be called 'unordered' attributes. There are various statistical techniques available for dealing with ordered attributes — several depend on scoring the categories and treating them as variables — but in general they will not be considered here.

A final pair of definitions is needed at this stage, *population* and *sample*. In statistical usage, the term population does not necessarily refer to people but is a technical term used to describe the complete group of persons or objects for which the results are to apply. A survey of motor cars in current use might employ a definition for the population as all cars with current registration licences. A study of overcrowding in London may define the population as all dwelling houses and flats in the Greater London area. A study of the incidence of poverty in old people might define its population as all persons aged over 65 in the United Kingdom. It is rarely possible to find out information for the complete population, so only a subset or sample of the population is investigated.

If the results for the sample are to apply to the whole population, it is essential that the sample to be studied should be carefully selected. Incomplete coverage of the population necessarily leads to error — the sampling error — because the sample cannot be expected to be exactly representative of the population. It is important to know the likely amount of such error for otherwise the sample results will be of uncertain value. If the sampling procedure is conducted such that every member of the population has a calculable (and non-zero) chance or probability of appearing in the sample, then statistical theory provides methods of estimating the likely value of the sampling error. But if the selection probabilities are incalculable, as in the case of quota sampling where the final choice of the persons in the sample is left to the interviewers (see Moser [16]), the sampling error cannot be estimated so that only a value judgement of the representativeness of the sample can be made. Here we shall confine our attention to sampling procedures for which selection probabilities can be calculated, called random or probability sampling, and moreover to the simplest kind — simple random sampling. Further consideration of simple random sampling and sampling errors is deferred until Section 3.

The distinctions and definitions made in this introduction will be employed throughout the following sections. Section 2 is concerned with the problem of summarizing statistical data and the distinction between attributes and variables is used. Section 3 introduces the notion of sampling error and discusses the logical basis and calculation of a confidence interval for dealing with sampling error in the descriptive part of a survey. Section 4 deals with the problem of sampling error in the analytic part of a survey; this is treated as an investigation of the existence of relationships and again the distinction between attributes and variables is employed.

2. SUMMARY STATISTICS

The first problem of statistical analysis is to summarize the information collected, so that it can be more readily comprehended.
The task is thus to reduce the data to some summary measures or
statistics, while still retaining the essential information. Attributes and variables will be discussed separately.

(a) Attributes

Table 1 shows the distribution of replies from a sample of prospective students at a university who were asked about their proposed degree subject.

Table 1. *Proposed Degree Subject of a Sample of 1200
Prospective Students at University X*

Proposed degree subject	Number of students
Arts	297
Mechanical Sciences	253
Natural Sciences	412
Social Sciences	88
Not stated	150
Total	1200

When dealing with only a sample of the population, we are
generally more interested in the proportion or percentage of the
sample giving each reply rather than the actual numbers involved.
In converting the actual numbers to percentages, there arises in
most surveys the problem of how to deal with the 'not stated'
group. Nothing is known about them so some assumption has to be
made, the usual assumption being that they are distributed between
the degree subjects in the same way as those who have responded:
for example, since 297 out of the 1050 (i.e. 28·3%) answering the
question replied 'Arts', we assume that 28·3% of the 150 not

answering the question would also have replied 'Arts' had they answered. When conducting a survey great care should be taken to minimize the 'not stated' group for, if it constitutes a substantial proportion of the sample and is not distributed as the remainder of the sample, a serious bias will result.

When presenting the results, in most cases the 'not stated' group should be removed from the sample and the percentages based on the total giving a classifiable response; the 'not stated' group should, however, be stated in the table in order to indicate the size of the possible bias. A suggested layout is shown in Table 2.

Table 2. *Proposed Degree Subjects of a Sample of 1200 Prospective Students at University X*

Proposed degree subject	Students
	%
Arts	28·3
Mechanical Sciences	24·1
Natural Sciences	39·2
Social Sciences	8·4
	100·0
Number of students stating subject	1050
Not stated	150
Total sample	1200

The size of the sample should be included in the table so that the reader can assess the results; other things being equal, results based on a sample of 120 students are liable to greater sampling error than those based on one of 1200 (see Section 3).

(b) **Variables**

As has been pointed out, variables can easily be transformed into attributes, and percentages can then be used to describe them (see Table 3), but there are other ways of summarizing variables.

Table 3. *Intelligence Scores for a Group of Students*

I.Q. Score	Students %
Under 120	3·9
120 —	20·3
125 —	41·6
130 —	27·1
135 and over	7·1
Total	100·0
Number of students	1508

Usually the main purpose is to measure the general level or central tendency of the figures and for this an average is used. There are a number of varieties of average, but discussion will be confined to the two most commonly employed, the arithmetic mean and the median. In fact, the arithmetic mean is nearly always used so that the term average or mean by itself usually implies the arithmetic mean. In algebraic terms the *arithmetic mean* (given the symbol $\bar{x}$) can be expressed as

$$\bar{x} = \frac{\Sigma x}{n}$$

where Σ means 'add together', x denotes the variable, and hence Σx means add together the values of the variable; n is the number of values in the addition. An obvious use of the arithmetic mean is a batsman's average in cricket: add together the number of runs obtained in each innings and divide by the number of innings (ignoring the problem of the times he was not out).

Suppose there are seven students who have 3, 1, 0, 2, 2, 4 and 1 A-level passes respectively, and we want to know the average number of A-level passes they possess. The arithmetic mean is

$$\bar{x} = \frac{\Sigma x}{n} = \frac{3 + 1 + 0 + 2 + 2 + 4 + 1}{7} = \frac{13}{7} = 1·86,$$

i.e. they have an average of 1·86 passes.

The simplification of a set of numbers to one summary figure, the arithmetic mean, may be too great a reduction for the mean tells nothing of the variability in the figures. Two batsmen, both with averages of 40, may have very different distributions of scores: one may be extremely consistent with scores ranging from 35 to 45, while the other may be erratic, scoring 0 on some occasions but 100 on others. We therefore need to measure the variation of the figures around the average: the appropriate index is the standard deviation for which the basic formula* is

$$s = \sqrt{\frac{\Sigma(x - \overline{x})^2}{n-1}}$$

though this is not the most suitable form for calculation purposes†. Consider the example above where the arithmetic mean was 1·86 A-level passes. The standard deviation is

$$s = \sqrt{\frac{1}{6}[(3-1\cdot86)^2 + (1-1\cdot86)^2 + (0-1\cdot86)^2 + (2-1\cdot86)^2 \\ + (2-1\cdot86)^2 + (4-1\cdot86)^2 + (1-1\cdot86)^2]}$$

$$= \sqrt{\frac{10\cdot86}{6}} = 1\cdot35$$

i.e. the standard deviation is 1·35 passes.

---

* In some textbooks a divisor of n rather than $(n-1)$ is given. If the standard deviation is calculated from a sample as an estimate of the population standard deviation, $(n-1)$ is the commonly used divisor. This is almost the case, so that the divisor of $(n-1)$ has been used here. However, if the size of the sample is large, there will be little difference between the two formulae. For a fuller discussion of the choice between n and $(n-1)$ see Bradford Hill [9].

† The reader interested in calculations should look at one of the

(continued on the next page)

If there were no variability in a set of figures, they would all be equal to their mean and hence their deviations from the mean would be zero, giving a standard deviation of zero: the more variable are the figures, the larger the standard deviation. For descriptive and other straightforward statistical uses, the standard deviation is the appropriate measure of variation since it is measured in the same units as the observations: in the above case, for example, the standard deviation is measured in terms of number of A-level passes. For more complex techniques, however, the square of the standard deviation, s^2, called the *variance*, has more suitable properties (in particular, see Section 4(c) on the analysis of variance).

The *median* is the most important alternative to the arithmetic mean as an index of central tendency. If the observations are placed in order of size, the median is the value of the middle observation. Ordering the A-level passes obtained by the seven students, we get:

$$0, 1, 1, 2, 2, 3, 4$$

The fourth observation is the middle one, and its value is 2; the median is therefore 2 A-level passes. The values of the observations one quarter and three quarters of the way up the ordered series are called the lower and upper quartiles respectively: here the lower quartile is 1 and the upper quartile 3. The mea-

---

standard textbooks such as Ilersic [10]. A formula more suitable for computational purposes is

$$s = \sqrt{\frac{\sum x^2 - \{(\sum x)^2/n\}}{n - 1}}$$

The use of working units can also considerably simplify the calculations.

sure of variability associated with the median is the *quartile deviation* or semi-interquartile range, which is defined as one half the difference between the values of the upper and lower quartile ; for these figures the quartile deviation is $\frac{1}{2}(3-1) = 1$ A-level pass. A problem arises in calculating the median when an even number of terms is involved, for there is then no middle term; the convention is therefore adopted of defining the median as half-way between the two middle terms. For example, the median of the ordered series 0, 1, 1, 2, 2, 3 is $1\frac{1}{2}$.

In general, the arithmetic mean is to be preferred to the median because it makes more efficient use of the observations ; in the mean the size of each observation is included, whereas in the median the size is only used to determine whether the observation is larger or smaller than the median. There are, however, some occasions when a few extreme observations — either comparatively very small or very large — may have an undue influence on the mean; on these occasions the median may be preferred. A typical example occurs with income distributions where one or two extremely high incomes exert a strong upward pull on the mean, but they do not have this effect on the median. Consider the following set of nine annual incomes : £800 £820 £900 £950 £1,000 £1,050 £1,100 £1,200 £10,000. The mean, highly influenced by the income of £10,000, comes out to be $\bar{x} = £1,980$: on the other hand the median, which is not so influenced by the extreme value, is £1,000. The median thus gives a better measure for the earnings of the 'average man'.

Mention must also be made of the use of graphical methods in presenting results. Surveys typically produce a large number of numerical results which, if they were all presented as tables or numerical indices, would make very tedious reading; diagrams are therefore often used to make the results more digestible. There are a number of graphical methods available — pie-charts, graphs, pictorial methods, etc. — which are described in most elementary texts*. Here attention is confined to the *histogram* or block

---

* See for example Moroney [15].

iagram which is used to illustrate the shape of a distribution.
Table 3 demonstrates that one method of dealing with variables is
o combine the scores into a small number of groups, and then use
ercentages to show the pattern of the scores. The histogram pro-
'ides an alternative graphical method of achieving this end. Consider the hypothetical data on heights of army recruits given in
Table 4: the percentages in column 3 give one way of showing
he distribution of heights, but it is difficult to get a clear pic-
ure, especially since the group-intervals in column 1 are of dif-
erent sizes.

Table 4. *Heights of a Sample of Army Recruits*

Height (1)	Number of recruits (2)	% (3)	Number of recruits per 1 in. of height (4)
5 ft.—	21	7·0	7·0
5 ft. 3 in.—	45	14·9	15·0
5 ft. 6 in.—	50	16·6	25·0
5 ft. 8 in.—	66	21·9	33·0
5 ft. 10 in.—	55	18·2	27·5
6 ft.—	48	15·9	16·0
6 ft. 3 in. but less than 6 ft. 6 in.	17	5·6	5·7
	302	100·0	

The histogram of these data given in Figure 1 shows much
more clearly the symmetrical shape of the distribution. The important point to note about the histogram is that the *areas* of the
blocks — not the heights — are proportional to the frequencies (number of recruits). Since the first and last two groups have intervals
of 3 inches compared with 2 inches for the middle groups, the
blocks of the outside groups are wider: in order to make the areas
of the blocks proportional to the number of recruits, heights are
plotted proportional to column 4 of Table 4, not column 2. Column
4 is obtained by dividing the number of inches in the interval into

the number of recruits in that interval.

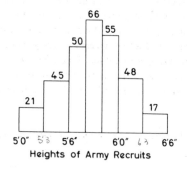

Fig. 1. *Histogram of Heights of Army Recruits*

As a second example, consider the hypothetical income distribution given in Table 5 and the corresponding histogram in Figure 2. Since each interval is a multiple of £250, it is convenient to plot heights of the blocks in the histogram proportional to the number of men per £250.

Table 5. *Incomes of a Sample of Men*

Annual income	Number of men	Number of men per £250
£250 –	110	110
£500 –	235	235
£750 –	336	336
£1,000 –	322	322
£1,250 –	250	250
£1,500 –	244	122
£2,000 –	134	67
£2,500 –	72	36
£3,000 –	46	23
£3,500 but less than £4,000	20	10
Total	1,769	

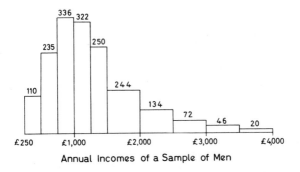

Annual Incomes of a Sample of Men

Fig. 2. *Histogram of Incomes of a Sample of Men*

Unlike the first example, this distribution is not symmetrical: a distribution with a long tail to the right is called *positively skewed*, and income distributions are frequently of this type. For completely symmetrical distributions, the arithmetic mean and the median have the same value, but for skewed distributions this is not so: with positive skewness, the median is less than the arithmetic mean and with negative skewness (i.e. a long tail to the left) the reverse applies.

The histogram is made up of blocks because the original data are grouped: Table 5, for example, only gives the number of men whose incomes fall within a given interval, not each man's exact income. If the sizes of these intervals were reduced, the width of the histogram blocks would become narrower and the diagram would probably become smoother: Figure 3 shows how the income histogram might look if intervals of £50 had been used in place of those of £250 and £500. Here, the scale cannot be indicated as in Figures 1 and 2 by writing frequencies on top of the blocks because the blocks are too narrow; instead an area scale has been added.

In the limit, the intervals would become so small that the histogram would appear as a smooth curve. In practice, of course, empirical distributions never become completely smooth because

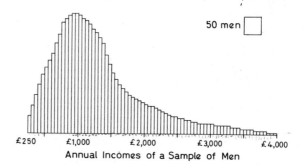

Fig. 3. *Histogram of Income Distribution Based on
Intervals of £50*

it is not possible to make the intervals infinitesimally small. On
the other hand, theoretical distributions derived from mathematical
statistics can in many cases be described by a smooth curve: this
applies to the normal distribution discussed in the next section.

3. SAMPLING ERRORS

In most research projects, the group of individuals selected for investigation does not comprise the complete group with which the research is concerned. We investigate only a sample of the population; the problem is then to generalize from the sample results to statements about the population. An enquiry may be designed to estimate the social class composition of students in technical colleges by studying a sample taken from the population of all such students. We would want to make statements about the population on the basis of the results obtained from the sample; for example, if 80% of the sample were classified as working class, we might infer that 80% of the population were working class. It is essential to be aware that this 80% is only an estimate of the population percentage: since it is calculated from a sample, it will in general not be identical with the population value. The distinction between sample estimates and population values is a basic one in statistical theory. For this reason, different symbols are employed for sample estimates which are denoted by letters of the Roman alphabet and population values which are given by Greek letters; for example, the sample arithmetic mean is denoted by $\bar{x}$, the population mean by μ; the sample proportion (or percentage) by p, the population proportion by π; the sample standard deviation by s, the population standard deviation by σ. Here it will be assumed that the difference between the sample estimate and the population value is only the result of sampling errors. In general, errors in survey research can be divided into sampling and non-sampling errors; the latter include errors due to clerical mistakes, interviewer bias and non-response*. Non-sampling errors will be assumed to be non-existent for the following discussion.

---

* See Moser [16] for a discussion of non-sampling errors.

Since the sample estimate and population value are usually different, it is necessary to know something about the difference. Ideally we would like to know the size of the difference, but this implies a knowledge of the population value, in which case no research is needed. But, while we cannot know the actual size of the difference for any particular survey, it is possible to estimate the average variability about the population value for all the possible samples that could have been taken from this population. This estimate of variability can only be made, however, if random (probability) sampling is used.

Here only the simplest type of random sampling — simple random sampling — will be considered. With this method every individual in the population has an equal chance of appearing in the sample; also, the chance of any one individual being chosen is independent of the chance of any other individual. Simple random sampling must not be confused with haphazard selection; the selection of a simple random sample is a precise and carefully planned operation which is described in detail elsewhere (e.g. Moser [16]).

As an illustration of the logical basis of sampling theory, consider the case of a simple random sample of size n being selected to give the sample mean $\bar{x}$ as an estimate of the population mean μ. Consider what would happen if the operation of taking a simple random sample of size n were repeated an infinite number of times (replacing the original sample each time before selecting the next one). The sample means would differ from one another but most of them would be somewhere near the true mean μ. Statistical theory can show that the distribution of sample means would look like the distribution shown in Figure 4.

The distribution in Figure 4 is extremely important in statistics and is known as the *normal distribution*.* There is, in fact,

---

* It is one of a number of sampling distributions that recur throughout statistical theory; the most important of the others are Student's 't' distribution, the variance-ratio or 'F' distribution, and the χ^2 distri-
(continued on the next page)

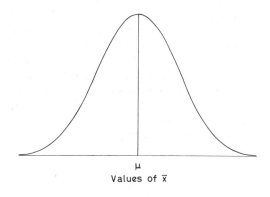

μ
Values of x̄

Fig. 4. *Distribution of Sample Means*

not just one normal distribution, but a whole family of them: to
specify any particular one, two measures must be given, a measure of the average and one of variation — the arithmetic mean
and standard deviation. The distribution of sample means will, in
general, not exactly follow, but only approximate to, a normal distribution. The closeness of the approximation depends on the shape of
the distribution of the original observations and on the size of the
sample: the nearer the distribution of the original observations is
to the normal distribution and the larger the sample, the closer will
be the approximation. For example, the histogram of heights of army
recruits (Figure 1) is fairly symmetrical and resembles the normal distribution, so the normal distribution is likely to be a satisfactory approximation to the sampling distribution of mean heights
even for small samples ; the income histogram (Figure 2) is, how-

bution. Applications of each of these distributions occur in later
sections.

ever, less like the normal distribution, and hence the normal distribution is likely to be a poor approximation to the sampling distribution of mean incomes if the samples are very small. In any event, the approximation is good enough for most practical purposes for samples of over 30, no matter what the shape of the original distribution. Since the normal distribution is specified mathematically, we can accurately state some of its properties: for example, if we measure 1·96 standard deviations either side of the population mean, then that range will contain 95% of the distribution; if 2·58 is substituted for 1·96 then 99% of the distribution is included (see Figure 5).

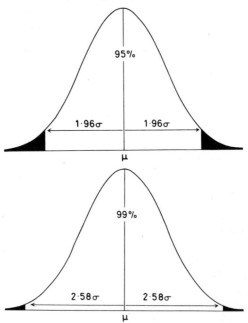

Fig. 5. *95% and 99% Intervals of the Normal Distribution measured about the Population Mean*

Since the sample means are approximately normally distributed, 95% of them will fall within a range of 1·96 standard deviations *of the sample means* about the population mean. Note that we are considering the distribution of sample means, not the distribution of the original observations, and hence we require the standard deviation of the sample means as our measure of variability; in order to distinguish it from the standard deviation of the original observations, the standard deviation of sample means is called the *standard error* of the mean (usually abbreviated to S.E.$_{\bar{x}}$). Since the standard error is the measure of variability in an infinite number of samples, it obviously cannot be calculated; moreover, in a practical situation we only take one sample and, since at least two values are needed before an estimate of variability can be made, we cannot even estimate it directly. But fortunately the standard error can be estimated indirectly by relating it to:

(i) The standard deviation of the original observations, S*. If every observation in the population had exactly the same value, i.e. $S = 0$, then the sample means for any selected samples would be the same, so that S.E.$_{\bar{x}} = 0$. The more variable the population, the larger is S.E.$_{\bar{x}}$.

(ii) The size of sample, n. It seems obvious that the larger the sample the closer on average the sample means will be to the population mean. This view is confirmed in the formula for S.E.$_{\bar{x}}$ where n appears in the denominator, so that the larger the value of n the smaller is S.E.$_{\bar{x}}$.

(iii) The proportion of the population covered, n/N, which is known as the sampling fraction. In fact, this factor is surprisingly unimportant; it can be ignored if the sampling fraction is less than 10%, a situation which occurs very often. It is the size of the sample itself, reflecting the amount of information collected, which is important in determining the accuracy of the results, not the proportion of the population

---

* Here it is convenient to define the population standard deviation by $S = \sqrt{\Sigma(x - \mu)^2/(N - 1)}$, where N is the population size, rather than by the more usual $\sigma = \sqrt{\Sigma(x - \mu)^2/N}$.

covered in the survey. In a number of situations, the
population is a hypothetical one of infinite size, in
which case the sampling fraction is infinitesimally
small.

The actual formula relating the standard error to these three
factors is

$$\text{S.E.}_{\bar{x}} = \sqrt{(1 - n/N)\frac{S^2}{N}}$$

As indicated above, the factor $(1 - n/N)$ — called the finite
population correction — can usually be ignored, and then the formula
simplifies to

$$\text{S.E.}_{\bar{x}} = \frac{S}{\sqrt{n}}$$

In practice, even this formula cannot be quantified because it
contains the unknown population standard deviation. If the sample
is larger than about 30, the sample standard deviation, s, is a sufficiently accurate estimate of S to permit the substitution of s for
S to be carried out without any further adjustment; if the sample
size is less than about 30, the substitution of s for S introduces
added sampling errors which cannot be ignored. For small samples
it is necessary to allow for these additional sampling errors by referring to another distribution, known as Student's 't' distribution,
in place of the normal distribution. For simplicity, we will confine
our attention to the large sample case based on the normal distribution; the following argument, however, applies equally to small
samples, except that a figure for the appropriate 't' distribution
replaces the 1·96 of the normal distribution. Even so, we are still
only able to make the statement that the range $\mu \pm 1·96s/\sqrt{n}$ contains 95% of the sample means, a statement which has no practical
value; we need to transpose it into a statement concerning a range
measured about the sample mean. Consider in Figure 6 every $\bar{x}$ in
the range $\mu \pm 1·96s/\sqrt{n}$, for example $\bar{x}_2$ and $\bar{x}_3$; for every such
$\bar{x}$ the range of $1·96s/\sqrt{n}$ measured about $\bar{x}$ will contain μ. For

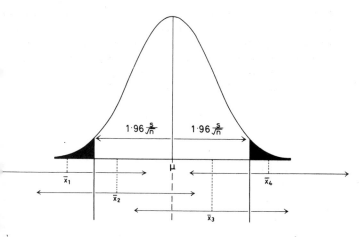

Fig. 6. *Ranges of 1·96 S.E.$_{\bar{x}}$ measured about Four Specimen Sample Means*

every $\bar{x}$ outside that range, e.g. $\bar{x}_1$ and $\bar{x}_4$, the range of $1·96s/\sqrt{n}$ measured about $\bar{x}$ will not contain μ. This is demonstrated in Figure 6, where the lines either side of the four specimen sample means are drawn of length $1·96s/\sqrt{n}$; the lines for $\bar{x}_2$ and $\bar{x}_3$ cross the middle vertical line, indicating the value of μ, while the lines for $\bar{x}_1$ and $\bar{x}_4$ do not do so. Furthermore we know that 95% of sample means fall within the range $\mu \pm 1·96s/\sqrt{n}$ and only 5% fall outside; therefore, for any particular sample mean, we can be 95% sure that the range $\bar{x} \pm 1·96s/\sqrt{n}$ contains the population mean. The range $\bar{x} \pm 1·96s/\sqrt{n}$ is called the 95% *confidence interval*; by altering the figure 1·96 to 2·58 the range becomes the 99% confidence interval. Any percentage probability level can be used and the appropriate figure can be obtained from tables of the normal distribution; the levels most commonly employed are, however, the 95% and 99% levels.

An example will illustrate the application of these ideas.

Suppose that a simple random sample of 64 students was taken to estimate the average number of marks obtained in O-level Mathematics by a particular group of 8,000 students. The arithmetic mean for the sample was 68·2 and the standard deviation 12·0. The effect of the finite population correction is negligible so that the standard error of the mean can be estimated by

$$\text{S.E.}_{\bar{x}} = \frac{s}{\sqrt{n}} = \frac{12 \cdot 0}{\sqrt{64}} = 1 \cdot 50 \text{ marks}$$

The 95% confidence interval is $\bar{x} \pm 1 \cdot 96 \text{ S.E.}_{\bar{x}}$, i.e.

$$68 \cdot 2 \pm 1 \cdot 96 \times 1 \cdot 50$$

or

$$65 \cdot 3 \text{ to } 71 \cdot 1 \text{ marks.}$$

In other words, it is 95% sure that the population mean, μ, lies within the range 65·3 to 71·1 marks. If it were felt that 95% certainty was not sufficient, the confidence interval could be widened to increase the level of certainty; the 95% confidence interval is the most commonly used but 99% confidence intervals are also employed. Here the 99% confidence interval is

$$68 \cdot 2 \pm 2 \cdot 58 \times 1 \cdot 50$$

or

$$64 \cdot 3 \text{ to } 72 \cdot 1 \text{ marks.}$$

An identical form of argument applies when interest centres on attributes rather than variables. In a simple random sample the percentage of persons with the attribute, p, is used to estimate the percentage for the population, π. If the size of the sample is large enough*, the hypothetical distribution of the infinite number

---

* The size of sample required for the distribution of sample percentages to be sufficiently close to the normal distribution depends on the
(continued on the next page

of sample percentages will closely approximate to the normal distribution. Again, let us confine our attention to large samples.

The standard error depends as before on a population value, in this case π. This is replaced by a sample estimate and the formula for estimating the standard error of a percentage (ignoring the finite population correction) becomes

$$\text{S.E.}_p = \sqrt{\frac{p(100 - p)}{n - 1}}$$

The 95% confidence interval is then $p \pm 1 \cdot 96 \text{ S.E.}_p$. For example, 36% of a simple random sample of 200 students are working class. The standard error of the percentage is given by

$$\text{S.E.}_p = \sqrt{\frac{36 \times (100 - 36)}{199}} = 3 \cdot 4\%$$

and the 95% confidence interval becomes

$$p \pm 1 \cdot 96 \text{ S.E.}_p = 36 \cdot 0 \pm (1 \cdot 96 \times 3 \cdot 4)$$

i.e.

$$29 \cdot 3\% \text{ to } 42 \cdot 7\%$$

Thus, with such a small sample, all we can say is that we are 95% sure that the population percentage lies within the range $29 \cdot 3$ to $42 \cdot 7\%$. If, as a result of the width of this range, the sample estimate is deemed too imprecise to be of practical value, the width of the confidence interval can (for the given confidence level) only

----

value of π; if π is near 50% the distribution is a close enough approximation to the normal distribution for much smaller sample sizes than if π is very small or very large (say less than 10% or more than 90%). A useful rough rule is that the normal distribution will be a satisfactory approximation providing $n\pi(100 - \pi)$ is greater than 100,000. For example, the normal distribution will be satisfactory if: π is about 10% and n exceeds 111; π is about 25% and n exceeds 53; π is about 50% and n exceeds 40.

be decreased by increasing the sample size. It must be noted, however, that the standard error formula is a function of the square root of the sample size; this means that a fourfold increase in the sample size will only reduce the width of the confidence interval by a factor of two (i.e. $\sqrt{4}$).

Before carrying out an enquiry, it is advisable to estimate the standard error for the suggested sample size to see whether the confidence interval will be small enough, or alternatively to estimate the size of sample necessary to give the required precision. Suppose that it is decided that the estimate of a percentage should be accurate to within $\pm 2\%$ (with 95% certainty), then the problem is to estimate the size of the sample necessary to satisfy this criterion. First, it is necessary to have some preliminary estimate of the percentage with the attribute, which may come from a pilot enquiry. The standard error is largest when $\pi = 50\%$, so that often this figure may be used to give the most conservative estimate of the required sample size. Let us take the figure of 50% in this case. We require

$$1 \cdot 96 \, \text{S.E.}_p = 2\% \qquad \text{where} \quad \text{S.E.}_p = \sqrt{\frac{\pi(100 - \pi)}{n}} \qquad *$$

Substituting $\pi = 50$, we get

$$1 \cdot 96 \sqrt{\frac{50 \times 50}{n}} = 2$$

so that

$$\sqrt{n} = \frac{1 \cdot 96 \times 50}{2} = 49$$

i.e.

$$n = 2401$$

---

* Since the formula is given in terms of π rather than p, the denominator is n rather than $n - 1$. This, however, is of little importance since it only leads to a difference of one in the estimate of the required sample size.

This means that a simple random sample of about 2400 persons is needed if we wish to be 95% sure that an estimate of a population percentage of about 50% is not more than 2% in error.

4. TESTING RELATIONSHIPS

Many surveys are concerned with testing hypotheses about the existence of associations, such as the hypothesis that high O-level Mathematics examination marks are associated with good performance in higher education. The sample results might suggest that the hypothesis is confirmed, but it is necessary to ensure that this confirmation represents something more than an artifact of the particular sample selected, i.e. is not just a result of sampling errors. In order to decide whether the association observed in the sample is an association which exists in the whole population, a statistical *test of significance* is needed. There is a wide variety of statistical tests; the aim here is to give only the general underlying theory, but a few of the most commonly used tests are described for illustration purposes.

In order to indicate the appropriate tests for particular situations it is useful to repeat the distinction between attributes and variables. Since tests of significance are concerned with comparisons, this involves three situations; comparisons can be drawn between

(i) *Attributes and attributes*

For example, is a person's mental health associated with his occupation? Is the type of crime committed by a criminal associated with the area where he was born? Is there an association between ownership of a car and type of employment?

In each of these cases, we are studying the relationship between two attributes: if more non-manual than manual workers have cars, or vice versa, then there is an association; if the proportion of the two groups having cars is the same, there is no association. This situation is discussed in Section 4(*b*).

26

(ii) *Variables and variables*

For example, is intelligence (measured by an intelligence quotient) related to age? Is income related to intelligence? Is a person's pulse-rate related to his temperature?

Each of these cases is studying the relationship between two variables. The discussion of this type of relationship is given in Section 4(c).

(iii) *Variables and attributes*

For example, is income related to type of employment? Do the marks obtained in an examination vary according to the method of tuition? Does the daily period spent watching television vary between children from different parts of the country?

Here we are studying the relationship between a variable and an attribute. The method of investigation is to compare the arithmetic means for the attribute categories; for example, to compare the average time spent watching television by children from each of the Registrar-General's ten standard regions of England and Wales.

The simplest example of this comparison is obtained when the attribute is a dichotomy; for example, is average income different for manual and non-manual workers? This type of case is discussed in Section 4(a). The more general case, where the attribute has more than two categories, is deferred until Section 4(d).

The comparison of two means is an example of the third group, but it will be useful to discuss this case immediately in order to explain the general principles involved in tests of significance.

(a) Significance Test for the Difference between Two Means

Suppose an enquiry was carried out to see whether arts and science students differ in their ages of entry to a particular university. A random sample of 100 students is selected from each of the two groups. The results are set out in Table 6.

Table 6. *Age at Entry to University X by a Sample of 100 Arts Students and 100 Science Students*

Age at entry	Arts students	Science students
16	10	7
17	18	12
18	36	31
19	19	24
20	14	16
21	3	10
Total	100	100

From the table it is not easy to compare the ages of the two samples. To simplify the comparison, the arithmetic means can be calculated. For the sample of arts students, the arithmetic mean is estimated as being

$$\overline{x}_A = \frac{\begin{array}{c}(16\frac{1}{2} \times 10) + (17\frac{1}{2} \times 18) + (18\frac{1}{2} \times 36) + (19\frac{1}{2} \times 19) \\ + (20\frac{1}{2} \times 14) + (21\frac{1}{2} \times 3)\end{array}}{100}$$

i.e.
$$\overline{x}_A = 18 \cdot 68 \text{ years}$$

(Note that students aged 16 are somewhere between 16 and 17 and have therefore been assumed to be aged $16\frac{1}{2}$, and so on.)*

Similarly the arithmetic mean for the sample of science students is estimated as

$$\overline{x}_S = 19 \cdot 10 \text{ years}$$

---

* This is an example of calculation of an average for a grouped frequency distribution; for details of the calculations, including methods of simplification, see an elementary textbook, for example Ilersic [10].

Thus there is a difference of 0·42 years in the average age of
entry of the two samples, but this does not necessarily imply a
difference in the averages for the two populations from which the
samples were selected; the difference between the two sample
values may be only the result of sampling fluctuations. It is to investigate this possibility that a test of significance is carried out.

The first stage is to specify the hypotheses. We set up a hypothesis, called the null hypothesis (symbolised by H_0), that there
is no difference between the two population means, i.e. the difference between the sample means is attributable solely to sampling
fluctuations. This can be expressed as

$$H_0 : \mu_A = \mu_S \text{ or equivalently } \mu_A - \mu_S = 0$$

It is also necessary to set up an alternative hypothesis (H_1) that
we will accept if we are forced to reject the null hypothesis. In
this example the most usual alternative hypothesis will be used,
namely that the two population means are not equal:

$$H_1 : \mu_A \neq \mu_S \text{ or } \mu_A - \mu_S \neq 0$$

It is possible to have other alternative hypotheses, such as one
stating that the mean age for arts students is higher than that for
science students ($H_1 : \mu_A > \mu_S$ or $\mu_A - \mu_S > 0$), so that the particular alternative hypothesis chosen is not as obvious as it might
at first appear. In a test of significance the null hypothesis is assumed true throughout the calculations until the final stage, when
it is rejected only if it is very unlikely to be correct. The procedure is to set up a model based on the assumption that the null
hypothesis holds, and reject the null hypothesis (i.e. accept the
alternative hypothesis) only if the data fit the model very poorly.
Thus a premium is placed on accepting the null hypothesis, and
this must be borne in mind when the test is interpreted.

If the operation of taking the two samples as above was repeated an infinite number of times and if for each occasion the

difference between the two sample means was calculated, then, as
for the distribution of sample means, the infinite number of differences would be approximately normally distributed for large sample
We assume the null hypothesis to be true so that the population
mean difference is zero, i.e. $\mu_A - \mu_S = 0$. The standard deviation
of the infinite number of differences, i.e. the standard error of the
difference between the means, is a combination of the standard
errors of the two means; in fact for large samples it is estimated
by

$$\text{S.E.}_{\bar{x}_A - \bar{x}_S} = \sqrt{\frac{s_A^2}{n_A} + \frac{s_S^2}{n_S}}$$

where s_A is the standard deviation of ages for the arts students
     n_A is the number of arts students
and s_S and n_S are the corresponding quantities for the science
     students. In this example $s_A^2 = 1 \cdot 583$ and $s_S^2 = 1 \cdot 838$, so th

$$\text{S.E.}_{\bar{x}_A - \bar{x}_S} = \sqrt{\frac{1 \cdot 583}{100} + \frac{1 \cdot 838}{100}}$$

$$= \sqrt{0 \cdot 03421}$$

$$= 0 \cdot 1849$$

Thus we have completely specified the model for the distribution
of differences: the differences are normally distributed, under the
null hypothesis the mean difference is zero, and the standard error
is calculated as $0 \cdot 1849$. The distribution is illustrated in Figure 7
    If an infinite number of sample differences were taken from
these populations and if the differences between the population
means were zero, then 95% of the sample differences would lie in
the range $0 \pm 1 \cdot 96 \, \text{S.E.}_{\bar{x}_A - \bar{x}_S}$, i.e. in the range from $- 0 \cdot 36$ to
$+ 0 \cdot 36$. Thus the difference between the two sample means will
exceed $0 \cdot 36$ for only 5%, or one in twenty, of the samples. In this

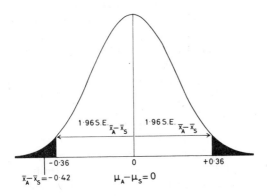

Fig. 7. *Distribution of the Differences between the Sample Means*

example, the difference, 0·42, does exceed that figure. One of two possibilities must apply : either the samples chosen are from that 5% of samples where the difference exceeds 0·36, or alternatively the null hypothesis, on which this model is based, is false. Since the former possibility is so unlikely, it is usual to accept the latter. But it is important to note that, if the null hypothesis were true, there would be a 5% chance of falsely concluding that there was a difference between the two population means. To reduce this chance, a higher level of significance than the 5% level can be employed; for example, under the null hypothesis, 99% of differences fall within the range 0 ± 2.58 S.E.$_{\bar{x}_A - \bar{x}_S}$, i.e. 0 ± 0.48.

If the observed difference were to exceed 0.48, it would be possible to say that there is a difference in the population means with only a 1% chance of reaching this conclusion if the null hypothesis were true. In this example the difference is less than 0.48, so that we cannot say that there is a difference at the 1% significance level.

If the actual difference had fallen inside the range for the 5% significance level (i.e. been less than 0·36), we would not have been able to reject the null hypothesis at that level ; furthermore, the 5% level is usually the lowest significance level employed. According to the argument this should result in the null hypothesis of no difference between the two means, being accepted. However, the conclusion should not be expressed in this way. When stating that there is a difference between the two population means, the chances of being wrong are known and fixed by the significance level used; when stating that there is no difference, the chances of being wrong are incalculable. Moreover, in many cases the actual difference may suggest that there is a true difference but may not be large enough compared with the standard error for the significance to reach the 5% level. In this example, a difference of only, say, 0.33 would not have been called significant, although the chance (when the null hypothesis is true) of a difference as large or larger than 0.33 is only $7\frac{1}{2}$% (only 3 times in 40). Thus, if the difference does not reach significance, the correct way to express the result is to say that there is not sufficient evidence to reject the null hypothesis or that the difference is not significant, rather than to say that there is no difference. Lack of significance is usually a negative result: it is feasible to prove that two things are different but virtually impossible to prove that they are equal.

Thus it should be realized that there are two types of error possible in a significance test. First, there is the Type I error which occurs when the null hypothesis is rejected when it is in fact true; the chance of this type of error is determined by the researcher's choice of significance level. Secondly, there is the Type II error which occurs when the null hypothesis is accepted when it is in fact false; the chance of this error is generally incalculable, and this is the reason why care is needed in presenting the result of not rejecting the null hypothesis. It should also be noted that the smaller the researcher makes the risk of a Type I error, the larger the risk of a Type II error becomes.

At this point it may be useful to summarize the steps involved in the above significance test. They are

1. Set up the null hypothesis, H_0, of no difference between the population means, i.e. $H_0: \mu_A - \mu_S = 0$

2. Set up the alternative hypothesis, H_1, to be accepted if H_0 is rejected. The alternative hypothesis employed was
$H_1 : \mu_A - \mu_S \neq 0$.

3. On the assumption that H_0 is true, construct a model for the sampling distribution of the differences $\bar{x}_A - \bar{x}_S$. The model is provided by statistical theory, in this case it was a normal distribution with mean zero and standard deviation estimated by

$$\sqrt{\frac{s_A^2}{n_A} + \frac{s_S^2}{n_S}}$$

4. Choose the significance level to be employed; the usual ones are the 5% and 1% levels.

5. Find the region of the model where H_1 is most likely to be true as compared with H_0. The size of this critical region is determined by the significance level chosen. Here the critical region comprised the two tails of the normal distribution, with $2\frac{1}{2}$% of the distribution in each tail.

6. Assess whether the sample difference $\bar{x}_A - \bar{x}_S$ falls in the critical region. In this example $\bar{x}_A - \bar{x}_S = 0.42$ did fall in the 5% critical region (but not the 1% region).

7. On the basis of the position of the sample difference make a decision:
   (a) If the sample difference falls in the critical region, accept H_1.
   (b) If the sample difference falls outside the critical region, come to no firm conclusion: on the basis of these samples, there is not sufficient evidence to reject H_0.

In this example, we accepted H_1 at the 5% level, and stated that there was a significant difference between the two means at that level of significance.

The steps outlined have been made specific to the problem considered, but the general procedure is the same for all significance tests.

(b) Testing for Association between Attributes

The simplest case of testing association between two sets of attributes occurs when both attributes consist of only two categories in this case the test becomes a test of significance of the difference between two proportions. For example, one attribute may be sex, the other poor eyesight measured by wearing glasses; the test for association assesses whether there is a significant difference between the proportion of males and females wearing glasses. There is a large-sample test of significance for difference between two proportions which follows closely the method outlined above for the test of the difference between two means; it is not intended to describe that method, but rather to consider an alternative, the χ^2 test, that can be generalized to situations where the attributes are not dichotomies. As an example of the test, we will consider the data in Table 7.

Table 7. *Marital Status Distribution of a Random Sample of Men and Women Undergraduates in University X*

	Men	Women	Total
Single	150	90	240
Engaged	50	50	100
Married	25	35	60
Total	225	175	400

From the sample data there does appear to be some association between the sex and marital status of the students, for 66·7% of the men are single compared with only 51·4% of the women. The question to be answered is whether this reflects a real difference between the population proportions or whether the difference could reasonably be explained by sampling fluctuations. The null hypothesis is that there is no association between the sex and marital status of all the students in University X; the alternative hypothesis is that there is some association.

On the basis of the null hypothesis a table of expected values is constructed. If there were no association between sex and marital status, the proportion of single students among the men and among the women would be expected to be the same : the best estimate of this proportion, obtained by combining the samples of men and women, is $240/400 \times 100 = 60.00\%$. Thus 60% of the 225 men would be expected to be single and also 60% of the 175 women, i.e. 135·0 men and 105·0 of the women. Similarly $100/400 \times 100 = 25\%$ of each group can be expected to be engaged, and $60/400 \times 100 = 15\%$ can be expected to be married. This then gives Table 8, which represents the model built on the assumption that the null hypothesis is true.

Table 8. *Expected Values*

	Men	*Women*	*Total*
Single	135·0	105·0	240
Engaged	56·25	43·75	100
Married	33·75	26·25	60
Total	225	175	400

Since the marginal totals of the expected value table are the same as those of the actual results, only two of the six figures in the middle of the table need to be calculated by multiplication and then the remainder can be obtained by subtraction. For example, once the expected values of 135 single men and 56·25 engaged men are calculated by multiplication, the remainder of the estimated values can be determined by the constraints of the marginal totals : since, of the 225 men in the sample, the expected number of single men is 135 and engaged men 56·25, it follows that $225 - (135 + 56.25) = 33.75$ must be the expected number of married men. Similarly, using the row marginal totals, it follows that there must be $240 - 135 = 105$ single women, $100 - 56.25 = 43.75$ engaged women, and $60 - 33.75 = 26.25$ married women. Since only two values in the table can be allotted freely — the rest being determined by the constraints of the marginal totals — the table is said to have two *degrees of freedom* (see below).

In order to assess whether there is an association, we must compare the actual figures obtained in the sample with the expected values of the model; the larger the difference between them, the greater the chance that there is a real association. The comparison between the actual and expected values is obtained by calculating the value of χ^2, given by the formula

$$\chi^2 = \Sigma \frac{(A - E)^2}{E}$$

where A represents the actual values and E the expected values as given in Tables 7 and 8.

$$\chi^2 = \frac{(150 - 135 \cdot 0)^2}{135 \cdot 0} + \frac{(90 - 105 \cdot 0)^2}{105 \cdot 0}$$

$$+ \frac{(50 - 56 \cdot 25)^2}{56 \cdot 25} + \frac{(50 - 43 \cdot 75)^2}{43 \cdot 75}$$

$$+ \frac{(25 - 33 \cdot 75)^2}{33 \cdot 75} + \frac{(35 - 26 \cdot 25)^2}{26 \cdot 25}$$

i.e.
$$\chi^2 = 10 \cdot 58$$

A large value of χ^2 implies a large difference between the actual and expected values, and hence suggests there is a real association; if χ^2 is small the association may be due to chance. The problem is to assess the meaning of 'large' and 'small' χ^2. The χ^2 test can be applied to tables of all sizes and since χ^2 is the sum of positive terms, it can be expected to be greater for larger tables because more terms contribute to the total. Thus the assessment of the size of χ^2 must take into account the number of cells in the table. In fact it can be shown mathematically that the relevant quantity is not the number of cells in a table, but rather the degrees of freedom. For the 2×3 table (i.e. a table with two columns and three rows) we have seen that once the first two expected values were calculated by multiplication the remainder were all determined by the constraint of the marginal totals, and thus 2×3 tables have two degrees of freedom. A general formula for the number of degrees of freedom (abbreviated to d.f.) in a table is $(C-1)(R-1)$ where the table has C columns and R rows ; for a 2×3 table this gives $(2-1)(3-1) = 2$ d.f. as above, for a 3×4 table there are $(3-1)(4-1) = 6$ d.f.

Returning to the example, we have observed a χ^2 value of 10·58 on 2 d.f. The significance of this value can be assessed by reference to a table of the χ^2 distribution (see, for example, Fisher and Yates [7]). For the χ^2 distribution with two degrees of freedom, the table shows that (when the null hypothesis of no association is true) the value of 5·99 is exceeded on only 5%, and the value of 9·21 on only 1%, of occasions. Since the value obtained, 10·58, exceeds 5·99 one of two alternatives must apply : either there is no association in the population and one of the 5% of χ^2 values which exceed 5·99 has occurred, or the null hypothesis is false. The probability of the first alternative is only 5%, i.e. 1 in 20, and therefore the second alternative is preferred. There is an association which is significant at the 5% level ; since 10·58 also exceeds 9·21, the association is also significant at the 1% level.

The method outlined for calculating χ^2 in a 2×3 table can be applied to tables with any number of rows and columns. The expected values and the values of χ^2 can be calculated in the same way, but the significance of χ^2 must, of course, be assessed by comparison with the tabulated value for the appropriate number of degrees of freedom. The table that occurs most often in practice is the 2×2 table with one degree of freedom ; here the test is a test of significance of the difference between two proportions.

The χ^2 test has a great many applications and, in fact, it is probably the most important test in survey research. There are, however, some limitations to its use. In the same sense that the normal distribution was only an approximation to the sampling distribution of means, so the theoretical χ^2 distribution is only an approximation to the sampling distribution of the quantity calculated as χ^2. Again, the larger the sample the better is the approximation. To determine whether the χ^2 test is applicable, the standard commonly set is that the expected value in every cell must be at least five, but this is too stringent. Cochran has found that, providing only a few cells have expected values of less than 5 (say only one cell in five), a minimum expected value of 1 is allowable (Cochran [2]). For 2 × 2 tables there is an exact test, Fisher's exact test, which should be used if the minimum expected value is less than five (see, for example, Maxwell [13]). For 2×2 tables with small samples, including those where the χ^2 test is inappropriate, tables of significance have been published (Finney *et al* [6]) so that no calculations need be performed*. Tables of the significance of differences between two percentages based on large samples have also been published (Stuart [21]).

A full non-mathematical description of the varieties of χ^2 test is given by Maxwell [13].

(*c*) Testing for Association between Variables

Suppose that the marks obtained by a group of candidates for two examinations are available and we want to discover whether there is a relationship between the two sets of marks; for example, does a candidate who scores highly on examination X also score highly on examination Y?

For simplicity, suppose we have a sample of only ten candidates; their marks on the two examinations are set out in Table 9. Appraisal of the marks suggests that there is a relationship, but this is more easily seen if the pairs of marks are plotted as points on a graph, called a scatter diagram. The scatter diagram for these marks is given in Figure 8 and it is clear that there is a relationship, though by no means a perfect one. Rather than rely

---

* The tables of Finney *et al* have been extended in Bennett, B.M. and Ho C. (1966) *Supplement to Tables for Testing Significance in a 2 × 2 Contingency Table*, Cambridge University Press, London.

Table 9. *Scores for 10 Candidates on Two Examinations*

Candidate	Exam X	Exam Y
A	16	16
B	17	19
C	15	14
D	19	20
E	5	7
F	6	11
G	8	13
H	10	8
I	11	10
J	13	12

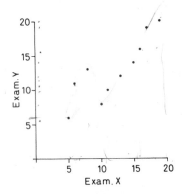

Fig. 8. *Scatter Diagram*

only on the scatter diagram, it is better to have a numerical index to measure the degree of relationship. Such an index is called a *correlation coefficient*.

There are several types of correlation coefficient but the one usually employed is the product-moment correlation coefficient, which measures how well the data fit a straight line. A perfect correlation would appear on the scatter diagram as shown in Figure 9(*a*); all the points fall on a straight line sloping upwards from left to right, indicating, for example, that a candidate with a high score on one examination will also have a high score on the other. Another example of perfect correlation is given in Figure 9(*b*) where again all the points fall on the straight line, but one

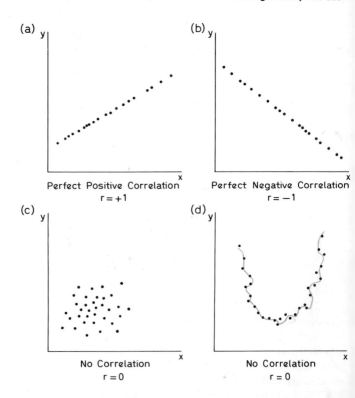

Fig. 9. *Scatter Diagrams showing Types of Correlation*

with a downward slope, so that high scores on one examination
are associated with low scores on the other. This is an inverse
or negative relationship where, for example, a candidate scoring
high in English scores low in Mathematics. In these situations,
if a candidate's score were known for only one of the examinations,
his score for the other could be predicted without error. If there
were no correlation between the two scores, the scatter diagram
would appear as in Figure 9(c); in this case, knowledge of one
score would be useless for predicting the other score. In Figure
9 (d) there is a clear relationship, but not a linear one. The product-
moment correlation coefficient is not suitable for non-linear relationships; in fact, in this example, it shows no correlation.

The formula for the product-moment correlation coefficient
is

$$r = \frac{\frac{1}{n-1} \Sigma (x - \bar{x})(y - \bar{y})}{\sqrt{\frac{1}{n-1} \Sigma (x - \bar{x})^2} \sqrt{\frac{1}{n-1} \Sigma (y - \bar{y})^2}}$$

where x is the score on examination X

y is the score on examination Y

$\bar{x}$ and $\bar{y}$ are the corresponding arithmetic means

and n is the number of candidates.

It should be noted that the denominator is the product of the
standard deviation of the x's and the standard deviation of the
y's; the numerator is called the covariance of x and y. While this
formula defines the correlation coefficient, it is not suitable for
calculation purposes and the following formula, which is mathematically equivalent to the one above, is preferable*

$$r = \frac{\Sigma xy - n\bar{x}\bar{y}}{\sqrt{(\Sigma x^2 - n\bar{x}^2)(\Sigma y^2 - n\bar{y}^2)}}$$

* The use of working units can add considerable further simplification.
  See, for example, Ilersic [10].

A correlation coefficient cannot lie outside the range from
-1 to $+1$: a value of $+1$ indicates a perfect positive correlation
as in Figure 9(a), a value of -1 a perfect negative correlation as
in Figure 9(b) and a value of 0 represents no correlation as in
Figures 9(c) and 9(d). The value of the correlation coefficient
for the data in Table 9 is $r = +0.85$, which shows a high degree
of positive relationship between the candidates' scores on the two
examinations.

The correlation coefficient estimates the degree of linear
relationship between the variables but it may be that the relationship observed only appears in the sample and does not, in
fact, exist in the complete population. This can be examined by
testing whether the correlation coefficient differs significantly
from zero, the null hypothesis being that the population correlation coefficient is zero. Let the alternative hypothesis be that
the population correlation coefficient is not zero. To carry out
the following test of significance it is necessary to assume that
both the x variable and the y variable follow normal distributions.
Consider the quantity

$$t = \frac{r\sqrt{n-2}}{\sqrt{1-r^2}}$$

If $r = 0$ then $t = 0$; if r is large and positive (i.e. near 1), t is large
and positive; if r is large and negative (i.e. near -1), t is large
and negative. Thus the null hypothesis of no correlation should be
rejected if t is large, positive or negative. The quantity 't' is
taken because, if the null hypothesis is true, it has a known
sampling distribution. This distribution is called Student's 't'
distribution and, like the χ^2 distribution, it depends on the number of degrees of freedom available, which for this test is $(n-2)$
where n is the number of pairs of observations. In this example

$$t = \frac{0.85\sqrt{8}}{\sqrt{1-(0.85)^2}} = 4.56$$

Referring to the 't' distribution with 8 degrees of freedom, it is found that the 5% significance point is given by $t = 2 \cdot 31$ and the 1% point by $3 \cdot 36$. We therefore reject the null hypothesis of no correlation at the 1% level of significance and conclude that there is some real relationship between the two sets of examination scores.

It has been shown that the existence of some correlation between two scores implies some degree of linear relationship. It is often useful to employ the correlation between two variables to predict one variable from a knowledge of the other; for example, if a candidate were absent from one examination, his missing mark could be estimated from a knowledge of his mark in the other examination. In terms of the scatter diagram, the method involves finding the straight line that provides the best fit to the points and then using the equation of this line and the knowledge of the 'x' score to predict the unknown 'y' score; the best-fitting straight line for predicting the 'y' score given the 'x' score is called the linear *regression* of y on x. This simple type of regression can be extended in two ways. First, if the relationship is not linear but perhaps of the form illustrated in Figure 9(d), then curvilinear regression can be used to fit the best fitting curve. Secondly, if a number of other measures are available to assist in predicting the 'y' score, they can all be included; this important extension is called multiple regression. Fuller discussions of regression are given by Quenouille [18] and Snedecor [19].

Before leaving the subject of correlation, mention should be made of *rank correlation* techniques. There are two main types of rank correlation coefficient, Spearman's ρ and Kendall's τ, which are both described in detail by Kendall [11]; here only a brief description of Kendall's τ will be given. Suppose that in place of the examination scores given in Table 9, we have only the relative positions, or rank order, of the candidates: the rank orders equivalent to the scores in Table 9 are given in Table 10, but the candidates have been re-arranged so that they are listed in order of their rank positions on examination X.

Table 10. *Rank Positions of 10 Candidates on
Two Examinations*

Candidate	Exam X	Exam Y
D	1	1
B	2	2
A	3	3
C	4	4
J	5	6
I	6	8
H	7	9
G	8	5
F	9	7
E	10	10

Since the candidates have been listed according to their ranking on examination X, we need only study ranking Y; if there were
perfect correlation, ranking Y would follow the same ordering. The
formula for Kendall's rank correlation coefficient is

$$\tau = \frac{2S}{n(n-1)}$$

where there are n candidates and S is calculated as follows. Take
each candidate in turn for ranking Y; add the number of persons
listed below the particular candidate who have rank positions
higher than he does and subtract the number who have lower ranks.
Perform this calculation for every candidate and add together the
resulting numbers to give the value of S. For example, consider the
contribution to S from candidate J : on ranking Y his position is 6,
listed below him are the four ranks, 7, 8, 9 and 10 which are
larger than 6, and one rank 5, which is less than 6. Candidate
J's contribution is thus $+4-1 = +3$. Taking each candidate in
turn, the value of S is given by

$$S = (9-0) + (8-0) + (7-0) + (6-0) + (4-1)$$
$$+ (2-2) + (1-2) + (2-0) + (1-0)$$

i.e. $$S = 35$$

and $$\tau = \frac{2 \times 35}{10 \times 9} = + 0.78$$

Note that, in this case, the value of Kendall's τ is similar to the value of the product-moment correlation, which was $+ 0.85$. For the problem of testing the significance of τ, the reader is referred to Kendall [11]. A common problem in ranking techniques is that of tied ranks; if several candidates obtain the same score on a test they should be given the average rank of the set of positions they take up. For example, if five scores were 6, 7, 7, 8, 9 the ranks would be taken as $1, 2\frac{1}{2}, 2\frac{1}{2}, 4$ and 5; the two scores of 7 take up the second and third positions and are therefore both ranked at $2\frac{1}{2}$. If there are relatively few tied ranks, this technique can be employed without further adjustment, but if the number of ties is appreciable an adjustment to the simple formula for a rank correlation coefficient is needed (see Kendall [11]).

(d) **Testing for Association between an Attribute and a Variable**
The simplest example of this kind of relationship, a large-sample significance test for the difference between two means, has already been described. If the samples are small, say less than 30, and if the standard deviations for each population can be assumed to be equal*, then the appropriate test of significance for the difference between two means is a 't' test, i.e. a test based on Student's 't' distribution. This test also assumes that the observations are normally distributed, but is fairly robust for departures from normality. It involves calculating a pooled estimate of the common standard deviation from the two samples, using the

---

* This assumption can be tested by a test based on the 'F' distribution; see, for example, Snedecor [19].

formula*

$$s = \sqrt{\frac{\Sigma(x - \bar{x})^2 + \Sigma(y - \bar{y})^2}{n_1 + n_2 - 2}}$$

where x's are the observations in one sample

y's are the observations in the other sample

n_1 is the size of one sample

n_2 is the size of the other sample

The standard error of the difference $(\bar{x} - \bar{y})$ is then given by

$$\text{S.E.}_{\bar{x} - \bar{y}} = \sqrt{\frac{s^2}{n_1} + \frac{s^2}{n_2}} = \sqrt{s^2 \left(\frac{1}{n_1} + \frac{1}{n_2} \right)}$$

(Note the similarity with the $\text{S.E.}_{\bar{x} - \bar{y}}$ for large samples; the only difference is that the single value s^2 replaces s_1^2 and s_2^2.) The test of significance then proceeds as for the large sample case except that the significance is assessed according to the 't' distribution with $n_1 + n_2 - 2$ degrees of freedom, rather than the normal distribution.

If the samples are small and the standard deviations are found to differ significantly, then the above method is not applicable. Instead, an approximate test has to be used: Cochran and Cox [3] provide one such test and Welch [22] another. (See Ferguson [5] for a description of both methods.)

The test of significance of the difference between two means can be extended to a test for the difference between several means ;

---

* The equivalent formula

$$s = \sqrt{\frac{\Sigma x^2 - n_1 \bar{x}^2 + \Sigma y^2 - n_2 \bar{y}^2}{n_1 + n_2 - 2}}$$

simplifies the calculations. Working units can add further simplification; see an elementary textbook for a discussion of working units.

this technique is called the one-way *analysis of variance*. The null hypothesis is that all the population means are the same, the alternative hypothesis that they are not all the same; if the alternative hypothesis is accepted, it could be that all the population means are different or that one differs from the others, which are all the same.

As an example of a one-way analysis of variance consider a comparison of three teaching methods based on three samples of students: the hypothetical results are given in Table 11.

Table 11. *Test Scores of Students Taught by Three Methods*

Scores of students taught by:

	Textbook only	Teaching machine only	Class tutor only
	w	y	z
	25	27	30
	22	26	27
	24	27	25
	24	24	26
	20	26	27
Mean	$\bar{w} = 23.0$	$\bar{y} = 26.0$	$\bar{z} = 27.0$

As with the 't' test, we must make the assumption that the standard deviations of the three populations are the same.* Under this assumption and if the null hypothesis (that the population means are the same) is true, we can make two estimates of the common population standard deviation, or rather variance (the square of the standard deviation) which is more amenable to mathematical treatment.

---

* This assumption can be tested by Bartlett's test, which is described by Snedecor [19]. If the standard deviations are significantly different, there are still methods of dealing with the problem; see, for example, Snedecor [19] on transformations.

One estimate can be obtained from the three samples pooled together in the same manner as for the '*t*' test. This provides an estimate s_1^2 of the population variance σ^2, where

$$s_1^2 = \frac{\Sigma(w - \bar{w})^2 + \Sigma(y - \bar{y})^2 + \Sigma(z - \bar{z})^2}{n_1 + n_2 + n_3 - 3}$$

In this simple example the samples are, of course, of equal size so that $n_1 = n_2 = n_3 = n'$ (say).

For the second estimate it is necessary to remember that the standard error of the mean is just another name for the standard deviation of the mean. Since we have three means we can estimate the variance of the mean directly by an application of the basic formula $s^2 = \frac{1}{n-1}\Sigma(x - \bar{x})^2$. Denoting the estimate of the variance of the means as $s_{\bar{x}}^2$, we have

$$s_{\bar{x}}^2 = \frac{(\bar{w} - a)^2 + (\bar{y} - a)^2 + (\bar{z} - a)^2}{3 - 1}$$

where a is the mean of the three sample means, i.e. $a = (\bar{w} + \bar{y} + \bar{z})/$ Now we also know that the standard error of the means is $\sqrt{\sigma^2/n'}$: therefore, by squaring, the variance of the means is σ^2/n'. Thus, $s_{\bar{x}}^2$ is an estimate of σ^2/n', and hence $n's_{\bar{x}}^2$ is an estimate of σ^2. Let us denote $s_2^2 = n's_{\bar{x}}^2$ as this estimate of σ^2.

Thus we now have two estimates of σ^2. s_1^2 is an estimate based on a pooling of the estimates from within the samples and hence does not depend on the null hypothesis. s_2^2 is an estimate of the variance based on the difference between the sample means and is only a valid estimate if the null hypothesis is true; if the null hypothesis is false (i.e. the population means differ), the variation between the sample means can be expected to be larger than the variation due to sampling fluctuations alone, which in turn means that s_2^2 will be an over-estimate of σ^2. Thus by comparing s_1^2 with s_2^2 we can assess the truth of the null hypothesis: if s_2^2 is much larger than s_1^2, then this suggests that the null hypothesis is false, while if s_1^2 and s_2^2 are similar in size or s_2^2 is smaller than s_1^2, then the null hypothesis is likely to be true. The manner of investigating the relative sizes of s_1^2 and s_2^2 is by taking the ratio s_2^2/s_1^2, and observing whether it is much larger than 1. This assessment of what is meant by 'large' is made by reference to the sampling distribution of the ratio of two independent estimates of variance, the 'F' or variance-ratio distribution: as with the χ^2 and 't' distributions, the 'F' distribution depends on degrees of freedom, but it has two sets of them, one for the numerator and one for the denominator of the ratio. The degrees of freedom are equal to the number in the divisor of the estimate of variance : thus, in this example, there are $3-1=2$ degrees of freedom for the numerator and $n_1 + n_2 + n_3 - 3 = 12$ for the denominator. From a table of the 'F' distribution, it is found that, when the null hypothesis is true, the value of $F = 3 \cdot 89$ on 2 and 12 degrees of freedom is only exceeded on 5% and $F = 6 \cdot 93$ only on 1% of occasions. The calculations give the following values

$$s_1^2 = \frac{16 + 6 + 14}{12} = 3 \cdot 000$$

and, since $a = 25\frac{1}{3}$, $\quad s_{\bar{x}}^2 = \frac{\left(-2\frac{1}{3}\right)^2 + \left(\frac{2}{3}\right)^2 + \left(1\frac{2}{3}\right)^2}{2} = 4 \cdot 333$

so that $\quad\quad s_2^2 = n's_{\bar{x}}^2 = 5 \times 4 \cdot 333 = 21 \cdot 67$

We thus have the two estimates of variance $s_1^2 = 3 \cdot 00$ and $s_2^2 = 21 \cdot 67$ so that the ratio $F = 21 \cdot 67/3 \cdot 00 = 7 \cdot 22$. Since this value exceeds the tabulated figure for the 1% level (6.93), the two variances are significantly different at the 1% level. By the argument above, this implies that the population means for the three groups are different at this significance level. Observe that, from this test, it is not possible to say whether all the teaching methods produce different means or whether two of them are the same ; it can only be said that they are not *all* the same.

The term used for this technique 'analysis of variance' is very appropriate, for the overall variance in the scores is being analysed. It is divided into two components : one is the variance within the samples ; the other is the variance between them. These provide two independent estimates of the population variance which can be compared. One estimate (the within-sample estimate) is independent of the null hypothesis of equal population means, while the other (the between-sample estimate) is dependent on it. The consistency of these two estimates thus provides a test of the null hypothesis.

The analysis of variance is an extremely important statistical technique, which can be applied to much more complex situations than the example given. Further applications will not be discussed in detail here but it is perhaps worthwhile to indicate one further stage, the two-way analysis of variance. Suppose a group of students in higher education is classified in two ways, according to the kind of school from which they came and according to their attendance (full-time, part-time, occasional) ; for example, one could be full-time from a grammar school ; another an occasional student from a grammar school ; and a third part-time from a secondary modern school ; etc. All the students are given a test and we want to find out whether the mean scores differ for students from different kinds of school, whether the mean scores differ for students of different types of attendance, or whether certain combinations of students of particular attendance categories from particular kinds of school score higher or lower than the rest. By dividing the overall variance of all the students' scores into a number of components, it is possible to test each of these hypotheses.

A particular example of the two-way analysis of variance is the analysis of *matched* samples. Throughout the discussion of tests of significance, we have implicitly assumed that the samples being compared were independently selected one from another. For the investigation of differences, however, the use of matching can increase the efficiency of an experiment ; for example, consider an experiment to investigate whether a drug gives car drivers added concentration. In the simplest design, two groups of drivers would be selected at random, the drug would be given to one group (the experimental group) but not to the other (the control group). The drivers would then be given a test to measure their powers of concentration: the difference between the average test scores of the two groups would indicate whether the drug had an effect and its significance could be tested by the '*t*' test described earlier. If, however, it were known that concentration varies by age, this extra information could be used to improve the efficiency of the experiment. One method to utilize the information would be by using matched samples: instead of selecting the control group completely at random, for each individual in the experimental group an individual of the same age is selected for the control group, the selection for the control group being at random from all those drivers of the given age. In such an experimental design, a paired comparison experiment, the matching or pairing by age, results in related, not independent, samples. The appropriate method of analysis is the two-way analysis of variance, with one classification being experimental versus control group, and the other classification being the particular pair from the set of pairs. In practice, the variation between the pairs being generally of little interest, the computations are usually simplified by using a test known as the related '*t*' test; nevertheless this is just a special case of the two-way analysis of variance.

The computations involved in two-way and more complex analyses of variance are lengthy and it is necessary to have a routine method of performing them; Brownlee [1] gives clear instructions for these computations. The analysis of variance is closely connected with the design of experiments (experiments of the type given as an example in this section rather than large-scale surveys). A book by Cox [4] provides a simple non-mathematical introduction to experimental design and Maxwell [14] shows the application of analysis of variance to some types of design.

5. CONCLUDING REMARKS

The main purpose of this discussion has been to give the reader some basic understanding of statistical ideas by means of a short account of some of the simpler and more commonly used techniques The treatment has been brief but it is hoped that sufficient detail is provided for the reader, when confronted with a straightforward statistical problem, to be able to decide on the appropriate method of analysis, and that he should then read a fuller discussion of the technique from one of the references. In particular, attention should be paid to the underlying assumptions of the method, for most methods involve a number of assumptions about the material. For example, the χ^2 test assumes large samples; the 't' test for the difference between two means assumes that the two population variances are equal and also that the variables are normally distributed; and the analysis of variance assumes that the variances are equal in each sub-group, that the variables are normally distributed within each sub-group, and — for the more complex designs — that the effects of different factors are additive. Another important assumption common to all the methods of statistical inference outlined here is that of simple random sampling, an assumption which does not hold for most large-scale surveys where in general more complex sampling procedures are employed. If the material fails to meet any of the assumptions, misleading conclusions could result from the misapplication of the technique. A further reason for consulting a textbook is to find the most suitable method of computation: survey analysis usually involves a considerable amount of statistical computation so that it is extremely desirable to reduce the calculations to their simplest forms.

Caution should also be exercised in the interpretation of statistical association. A significance test may show that the association observed in a sample cannot reasonably be accounted for by sampling fluctuations, but it tells nothing of the *cause* of the association. A significant association may be found between a measure of a man's success at his job and his attitude to the work. His attitude may influence his degree of success, but equally well his success could influence his attitude. A further alternative is that some third factor — perhaps ability to do the work — influences both his success and his attitude. Therefore, no causal inference can be made solely on the basis of an observed association.*

Finally, a word should be said about obtaining statistical assistance. Survey research requires expertise in a number of fields — for example, the subject matter of the project, questionnaire design, methods of analysis and statistical techniques — and these skills rarely all exist in one person: ideally, therefore, survey research is conducted by a team of specialists, one of whom is a trained statistician. In practice, for financial or other reasons, it is often impossible to form such a team. One or two researchers must try to master all the skills, perhaps with some outside specialist assistance; frequently part of this specialist advice comes from a statistician. No matter, however, whether the statistician is part of the research team or merely an adviser on specific problems, the time to approach him is at the beginning of the project; too often his advice is not sought until the analysis stage, by which time it is usually too late to correct errors in the research design. Although this discussion has been confined to statistical analysis, the stages of design and analysis of research projects are closely inter-related; statistical expertise is also needed for the efficient design of experiments and surveys.

---

* See Moser [16] for further discussion of this point.

BIBLIOGRAPHY

[1] Brownlee, K.A. (1957). *Industrial Experimentation.* 4th ed. Her Majesty's Stationery Office, London. Provides useful instruction in methods of calculation, especially for analysis of variance.

[2] Cochran, W.G. (1954). *Biometrics,* **10**, 417-51. An article describing methods of strengthening the ordinary χ^2 test in certain situations.

[3] Cochran, W.G. and Cox, G. (1957). *Experimental Designs.* 2nd ed. Wiley, New York. A textbook on the analysis of experiments.

[4] Cox, D.R. (1958). *Planning of Experiments.* Wiley, New York. A lucid non-mathematical account of the principles (but not the analysis) of experimental designs.

[5] Ferguson, G.A. (1959). *Statistical Analysis in Psychology and Education.* McGraw-Hill, New York. A non-mathematical textbook of statistical methods.

[6] Finney, D.J., Latscha, R., Bennett, B.M. and Hsu, P. (1963). *Tables for Testing Significance in a 2 × 2 Contingency Table.* Cambridge University Press, London. Useful tables for testing the significance of a difference between two proportions when the samples are small.

[7] Fisher, R.A. and Yates, F. (1963). *Statistical Tables for Biological, Agricultural and Medical Research.* 6th ed. Oliver and Boyd, London. A book of statistical tables, but also contains some useful methods.

[8] Hays, W.L. (1963). *Statistics for Psychologists.* Holt, New York. A useful text concerned with principles as well as methods. It covers a wide range of techniques.

[9] Hill, A. Bradford (1961). *Principles of Medical Statistics.* 7th ed. Lancet, London. An excellent introductory text.

54

[10] Ilersic, A.R. (1964). *Statistics*. H.F.L. (Publishers), London. Provides a straightforward introduction to statistics and also discusses sources of official statistics.

[11] Kendall, M.G. (1962). *Rank Correlation Methods*. 3rd ed. Charles Griffin, London. A book containing both theory and methods of rank correlation techniques.

[12] Kish, L. (1965). *Survey Sampling*. Wiley, New York. An excellent account of the design and analysis of sample surveys.

[13] Maxwell, A.E. (1961). *Analysing Qualitative Data*. Methuen, London. An excellent non-mathematical account of varieties of χ^2 test.

[14] Maxwell, A.E. (1958). *Experimental Design in Psychology and the Medical Sciences*. Methuen, London. An account of experimental designs with particular reference to psychological experiments. It provides a useful account of the rationale of analysis of variance.

[15] Moroney, M.J. (1956). *Facts from Figures*. 3rd ed. Penguin Books, London. A useful Pelican introduction to statistics, but with a bias towards industrial applications.

[16] Moser, C.A. (1958). *Survey Methods in Social Investigation*. Heinemann, London. A book on survey methods, with chapter 5 giving a clear explanation of the ideas of sampling error.

[17] Mueller, J.H. and Schuessler, K.F. (1961). *Statistical Reasoning in Sociology*. Houghton Mifflin Company, Boston. A useful introductory text.

[18] Quenouille, M.H. (1952). *Associated Measurements*. Butterworth, London. A non-mathematical but advanced text on statistical methods.

[19] Snedecor, G.W. (1956). *Statistical Methods*. The Iowa State College Press, Iowa. A non-mathematical but advanced text on statistical methods.

[20] Stuart, A. (1962). *Basic Ideas of Scientific Sampling.*
      Charles Griffin, London. A book mainly on sample
      designs, with the first nineteen sections giving an
      excellent non-mathematical introduction to statistical
      inference.

[21] Stuart, A. (1963). *Applied Statistics,* **XII,** 87 - 101. An
      article giving tables for testing the significance of the
      difference between two percentages based on large
      samples.

[22] Welch, B.L. (1938). *Biometrika,* **29,** 350-361. An article
      giving a test for the difference between means when the
      population variances are unequal.

Alternative hypothesis, 29
Analysis of variance, 47-51, 52
  one-way, 47-50
  two-way, 50-51
Analytic surveys, 2
Arithmetic mean, 7-8, 28
  compared with median, 10, 13
  confidence interval for, 16-22
  tests of significance for, 27-33,
    45-51
Attributes, 2-3
  summary statistics for, 5-6
Average 7. See also arithmetic
  mean and median

Bartlett's test, 47n
Between-sample estimate of vari-
  ance, 50
Block diagram see histogram

Chi-square (χ^2) distribution, 37
Chi-square (χ^2) test, 34-38, 52
Confidence intervals, 2
  for means, 21-22
  for proportions, 22-24
Control group, 51
Correlation coefficient, 39
  product-moment, 39-43
  rank, 43-45
Covariance, 40
Critical region, 33

Degrees of freedom
  in χ^2 test, 36-37
  in 't' test of correlation coeffi-
    cient, 42
  in 't' test of difference between
    means, 46
  in 'F' test, 49
Descriptive surveys, 2
Expected values in χ^2 test,
  34-36, 38

Experimental design, 1n, 51

'F' distribution, 49
Finite population correction, 20

Graphs, 10

Histogram, 10-14
Hypothesis testing see Tests of
  hypotheses

Kendall's rank correlation coefficient, 43-45

Lower quartile, 9

Matched samples, 50-51
Median, 9-10
  compared with arithmetic mean,
    10, 13
Multiple regression, 43

Negative skewness, 13
Non-sampling errors, 15
Normal distribution, 16-19
  as distribution of difference
    between two sample means, 30
  as distribution of sample means,
    20-21
  as distribution of sample propor-
    tions, 22-23
'Not stated' group, 5-6
Null hypothesis
  in χ^2 test, 34
  in one-way analysis of variance,
    47
  in test of difference between two
    means, 29, 32
  in 't' test of correlation coeffi-
    cient, 42

Paired comparison experiment, 51
Percentage, 5-6, 6-7. See also
  proportion

Pie charts, 10
Population, 3, 15
Population value, 15-16
Positive skewness, 13
Probability sampling *see* random sampling
Proportion 5. *See also* percentage confidence interval for 22-25
tests of significance for 34-38

Quartile deviation, 10
Quota sampling, 4

Random sampling, 4, 16
Rank correlation, 43-45
Ranks, 43-44, 45
Regression, 43
Related 't' test, 51

Sample, 3, 15
Sample design, 1, 2
Sample estimate, 15-16
Sample size
and normal approximation, 17-18
estimating, 24-25
related to sampling error, 23-24
Sample survey design, 1n
Sampling distribution, 16n, 17-18
Sampling error, 3-4, 15-25
Sampling fraction, 19-20
Scatter diagram, 38-39
Semi-interquartile range, 10
Significance level, 31-32
Significance tests *see* tests of significance
Simple random sampling, 4, 16, 52
Skewed distributions, 13
Spearman's rank correlation coefficient, 43
Standard deviation 8-9. *See also* variance
Standard error
of difference between two means, 30, 46

of a mean, 19-20
of a proportion, 23
Statistic, 5
Student's 't' distribution *see* 't' distribution

't' distribution
and confidence interval for a mean, 20
and test of a correlation coefficient, 42
and test of the difference between two means, 45-46
Tests of hypotheses 1-2. *See also* tests of significance
Tests of significance, 2
analysis of variance, 47-51
and causation, 53
Chi-square (χ^2) test, 34-38
of a correlation coefficient, 42-43
of difference between two means, 27-33, 45-46
summary of steps involved, 32-33
't' test
of a correlation coefficient, 42-43
of the difference between two means, 45-46, 52
Type I error, 32
Type II error, 32

Upper quartile, 9

Variables, 2-3
summary statistics for, 6-14
association between, 38-43

Variance, 9, 47. *See also* analysis of variance

Variance-ratio ('F') distribution, 49

Within-sample estimate of variance, 50